LORD
HEAR OU

Intercessions and Meditations,
for use in public worship
and private prayer.

TED BURGE

Foreword by Bishop Robin Woods

The Canterbury Press
Norwich

First published 1991 by
The Canterbury Press Norwich
(a publishing imprint of Hymns Ancient & Modern Limited,
a Registered Charity)
St Mary's Works, St Mary's Plain,
Norwich, Norfolk, NR3 3BH

British Library Cataloguing in Publication Data

Burge, Ted
Lord of all, hear our prayer.
I. Title
264.035

ISBN 1–85311–046–9

Typeset by Cambridge Composing UK Limited
and printed in Great Britain by
St Edmundsbury Press, Suffolk

Foreword

by The Rt Revd Robin Woods, KCMG, KCVO

Stated with an elementary simplicity, entering into a time of prayer is comparable with preparing for a session with a photographer. He asks his subject to sit still, to look up and to smile. The living God is our photographer, ready to record ourselves, our circumstances and our hopes, with his infinite capacity to do so. It is indeed a constant wonder that in Christ he touches not only each individual in our immediate circle but also every society and nation existing in the sphere of his creative love. Although he is aware of our needs, he bids us to make supplication to him, whereby we express our confidence in him and our willingness to receive.

In so many areas of the world there are crises and violence, and in our own nation there is controversy and disunity. It is therefore even more important that Christ should find in his Church individuals and congregations lifting up their needs in prayer, with insight and intelligence. Worldwide conflicts and local relationships challenge our faith and our Christian loyalty. We need to look up with a confidence that comes from taking care with our intercessions and from being more attentive in forming our prayers and meditations.

Prayer is an event, sometimes regular, sometimes spasmodic, but the occasion requires help and preparation. Professor Ted Burge has set on their way those who, at home or in Church, want to pray with their minds alert and with understanding. We can be thankful that the Spirit has opened up the opportunity for laity and clergy alike to lead in public prayer and thereby share their personal experience with a wider circle. The wording of our prayers is however never easy. In this book we have substantial help from one who is acquainted with the ways of thought of today's believers and who has a wide knowledge of the secular and technological world. With his experience as a scientist of standing, he shares with us his ability to express our hopes and fears with a refreshing sympathy. Founded on his conviction that the Lord is ever with us, these intercessions and meditations give a vivid revelation of a natural eagerness to commune with God and to await his assistance.

Preface

THESE PRAYERS had their origin in the Intercessions led by lay men and women at the Family Communion of St Andrew's Church in Oxshott, Surrey. Other prayers were added as occasion persuaded me to write, and sometimes for the joy in perplexity of striving to know God more fully.

The seventy prayers in Part One cover seven subjects that are found in almost all worship. They were prepared for use with *The Alternative Service Book* (p. 125), and most of them have been used in public worship. It is hoped that they will be of value to all those who are asked to lead intercessions in their local church or group.

The sixty prayers and meditations of Part Two are arranged in seven sections, but many of the prayers could be placed in more than one section. One person's private meditation can be another's public prayer, therefore no attempt is made to distinguish between them.

The introductory prayer (on page 1) summarises much of my conscious purpose in writing this book. From time to time, I have tried to introduce accepted conclusions and terminology of modern science in relation to the creation of the universe and mankind. This is not because I believe these conclusions to be eternally correct or complete. It is because we must be able to express our faith and our theology in the contemporary idiom if we are to establish a rapport with the widely informed present generation. As far as possible we must use expressions that are, in modern terms, correct and logical, especially when speaking of the Christian's central beliefs in Creation, Death and Sin, and in Incarnation, Resurrection and Salvation.

With firm conviction I include miracles and mysteries. The ultimate truth will often be a paradox, with God at one of its poles, and mankind at the other. And in glorying in the paradox, and by immersion in the mystery, we enrich our worship.

E. J. Burge

Preface

Contents

Foreword by The Rt Revd Robin Woods iii
Preface v
Acknowledgements x
An introductory prayer 1

PART ONE: INTERCESSIONS 3
Preface to Intercessions 5
1. **Introduction** 7
2. **The Church** 9
3. **The State** 14
4. **Our neighbours** 19
5. **The sick** 23
6. **The dead** 27
7. **Commendation** 31

PART TWO: PRAYERS AND MEDITATIONS 35
Preface to Prayers and Meditations 37
8. **Experience** 39
   (a) Senses 39
   (b) Beauty 40
   (c) Enjoying creation 41
   (d) Science 42
   (e) Wood 43
   (f) Stone 44
   (g) Water 45
   (h) Needs 46
   (i) Silence 47
   (j) Sleep 48

9. **Belief** 49
   (a) Faculties 49
   (b) The Way, the Truth and the Life 50
   (c) Glory 51
   (d) Choosing 52
   (e) Children of our time 53
   (f) Creation 54
   (g) Evolution 55

(h) Survival of the fittest 56
(i) Sin and death 57
(j) Life after death 58
(k) Freewill 59
(l) Hallowed be your name 60
(m) Other religions 61
(n) May I be sure 62
(o) On the other hand 63
(p) Humility 64

10. Suffering 65
(a) Suffering 65
(b) Temptation 67
(c) Discontent 68
(d) Sleeplessness 69
(e) Hunger 70
(f) Depression 72
(g) Ups and downs 73

11. Relations 74
(a) Loving my neighbour 74
(b) Families 76
(c) Forgiving 77
(d) Money 78
(e) Rich and poor 79
(f) Love and joy 80

12. At Communion 81
(a) Easter Day 81
(b) Sacrifice 82
(c) The New Covenant 84
(d) Bread 85
(e) Wine 86
(f) Crosses 87

13. Occasions 88
(a) Nature conservation 88
(b) The balance of nature 89
(c) Recreation 90
(d) Musical talent 91
(e) Computers 92

(f) The Olympics 93
(g) Moving house 94

14. Groups 96
(a) Opening a discussion group 96
(b) Closing a discussion group 97
(c) Opening a Bible study 98
(d) Closing a Bible study 100

ACKNOWLEDGEMENTS

Many friends have contributed to this book by their comments and encouragement. In particular, I wish to thank my wife, Elizabeth, and also Sheepscombe friends Marie and Martin Oliver, and Oxshott teacher and poet Hilary Elfick. In the preparation for publication, Bishop Robin Woods has given kind interest and support which has been much appreciated. The final result is explicitly an expression of my trust, belief and hope-filled openmindedness, and any infelicities are likewise my own.

T.B.

An Introductory Prayer

Thoughts and Words

Lord of all,
 hear our prayer
 and guide us when we meditate.

Forgive us for so often burying you
 in obscure and out-moded
  thoughts and words.

Grant us grace,
 for the sake of those who know you not
 and for our children and our friends,

that our thoughts and words about you may be

not only
 helpful in their simplicity,
 healing in their loving-kindness
and heaven-sent in their joyfulness,

but also
 heartening in their vividness,
 humble in their science
and hallowed in their meaning,

and may unite us
 in the fulness of the resurrection life
  of your Church.

PART ONE

Intercessions

Preface to Intercessions

Ten prayers are presented here for each of the seven subjects in the paragraphs of the Intercessions at Holy Communion Rite A on page 125 of *The Alternative Service Book 1980.*

1. Introduction.
2. The Church.
3. The State.
4. Our neighbours.
5. The sick.
6. The dead.
7. Commendation.

In addition these prayers may be used in conjunction with other services and service books which include intercessions on these subjects.

In preparing these intercessions for general use, it has been necessary to remove many references to local and topical issues. This is a great pity. Such issues are our daily concern. They bring a healthy relevance to our worship, and should be introduced wherever appropriate in accordance with the occasion.

Several of the paragraphs cover such a range of topics that the lengths of the prayers given here sometimes prevent the use of all seven subjects, especially when local and topical issues are inserted. Therefore some suggestions for abbreviations are indicated by square brackets.

1. Introduction

Almighty God, our heavenly Father,
you promised through your Son, Jesus Christ,
to hear us when we pray in faith.

1(a) Grant us, we beseech you,
grace to continue steadfast in faith,
  to experience the dynamic of hope,
  and to practise the mystery of your love.

1(b) Grant us grace to commune with you,
that our thoughts
  may become your thoughts,
and that our silence
  may be filled with your peace.

1(c) Reassure us when our faith seems weak,
and protect us from presumption
  as we approach your throne.

1(d) Teach us, good Lord, to pray aright,
that we may be
  in tune with your will,
  in harmony with one another,
  and at peace in our hearts and minds.

1(e) Help us to listen to your Holy Spirit,
  to know the purpose of our being,
  and in penitence to be endowed
    with the means of our salvation.

1(f) Open our minds
  and win our hearts,
that our thoughts, affections and wills
  may be pure, robust and joyful
    and forever forgiving.

1(g) We thank you for fulfilling your promises.
Help us to continue to watch and pray,
that we enter not into temptation,
for all such things
are possible with you.

1(h) Guide us in our prayers,
that we may conform to your will,
come to know you more truly,
love you more purely,
and glory in your presence.

1(i) Put the right thoughts in our minds,
that we may speak heartfelt words,
and hear your message to us.
Lift our souls to praise you for your goodness,
and purify our zeal for your Church.

1(j) Shape and colour our prayers,
so that they and we may mirror your image.
Reveal to us your will,
and grant us grace and wisdom
to know our weaknesses
and our strengths.

Lord, in your mercy
Hear our prayer.

2. The Church

2(a) Strengthen, O Lord, the leaders of your Church,
that they may see you eye-to-eye,
and be one within – and between – themselves.
Grant us, with them, grace to grow together
in the practice of hallowed fellowship,
that in hearing your word
we may be made aware,
in seeing the needs of others
we may remember your commands,
and in doing your will
we may understand,
become united in your truth,
and by the well-timed inspiration of your grace
reveal your glory in the world.

2(b) Your Church, O Lord, is all around us,
and we are but a few of its members.
In togetherness and joy we thank you
for the riches of your revelation.
Help us to be aware of the unity of your truth
that binds us together and to you.
[Strengthen each one of us, bishops, priests,
deacons and all manner of laity,
that we may serve you with all we possess.]
May your Holy Spirit guide us day by day,
along paths both well trodden and new struck,
that thereby your glory may be revealed
in all the world.

2(c) Strengthen (*N.*) our bishop,
and all your Church,
in the service of Christ,
that even as John the Baptist
prepared the way for the Word-made-flesh,
so also we may be voices
crying in the wilderness
of this world's unbelief.
[Grant that those who confess your name
may be united in your truth,
and let the love of truth,
and the truth of living together in love,
help them to reveal your glory in the world.]

2(d) Strengthen, O God, (*N*) our bishop,
and all your Church,
in the service of Christ.
Give grace to us all, whatever our calling,
that we may through the words of scripture
resonate with the disciples and brethren
of the early Church,
and find rapport with the prophets and priests
of the old covenant,
through the perfect sacrifice of Christ,
the high priest of all our blessings.
[May those who confess the name of Christ
be united in your truth,
live together in your love,
and reveal your glory in the world.]

2(e) We pray for the Church, the body of Christ,
for bishops and those who select them,
for priests and deacons
and those who train them,
for all those laity who hold office,
for those who serve in whatever capacity,
and for those who in unseen and untold ways
contribute to the life and growth
of your Church.
[And we thank you Lord for all the devoted service
given and enjoyed by both laity and clergy,
who live together in your love,
and reveal your glory in the world.]

2(f) Defend, O Lord, your Church
with the weapons and armour
of your Holy Spirit,
that in all attacks and temptations to evil
we may share in the victory of your Cross.
When faith is infiltrated with doubt,
muster our reserves,
and rally your saints on Earth
and in Heaven,
to our assistance.
And when hope is high,
and we are amazed by your grace,
give us thankful hearts,
and keep us alert to the needs of others.

2(g) Strengthen (*N.*) our bishop,
and (*M.*) our parish priest,
and all the clergy of your Church.
Bless their preaching and teaching,
and their pastoral care,
with wisdom, faith and love.
[Let not the administration
that laymen can and ought to do
steal the time and concern needed by the clergy
to exercise their spiritual gifts.]
In unity of worship,
reveal to us the unity of truth,
and the sanctity of love,
that your glory may be revealed
in this parish,
and in all the world.

2(h) Strengthen, O Lord, your Church,
where most it needs new strength.
Where faith is faint,
and zeal is weak,
unite us in your truth,
and quicken our love for you
and for each other.
Focus our attention in preaching and prayer,
and in teaching and witness,
on the words and images we use,
that we may communicate more convincingly
the central features of our faith,
and thereby reveal
your glory in the world.

2(i) Give grace, strength and clarity of vision
to (*N.*) our bishop,
and to all clergy and laity.
Inspire us to work together in love with you,
towards the salvation of mankind,
within the fellowship of your Church.
Unite us in truth,
in humble receptiveness of mind and heart,
through every channel of revelation,
that by living out the truth,
and following your example,
we may reveal your glory
to all around us.

2(j) Strengthen for service, Lord,
all members of your Church,
not only the leaders,
but also the led.
Help us all to exercise our gifts,
by the indwelling of your Holy Spirit,
without let or hindrance,
that the richness of your uniting truth
may bring us to the life and love,
and the peace, joy and hope,
that reveal your glory
in the world.

Lord, in your mercy
Hear our prayer.

3. The State

3(a) Bless, O Lord, Elizabeth our Queen
and inspire her ministers,
that in the affairs of State she may be guided,
and this realm ruled,
in the paths of wisdom and benevolence.
In your mercy reveal justice and truth
to those in authority,
that those who are under authority
may labour in pleasure and peace,
and that each may honour the other.
Help us to seek the common good and find therein
the legitimate well-being
of conflicting interests;
in industrial problems,
in racial prejudice,
in national self-seeking,
and in international disputes.
Help us, O Lord, to be faithful in small things
and thereby make manageable
the larger issues.

3(b) Lord of Lords, King of Kings,
in whom alone is true security,
defend our Sovereign Queen Elizabeth,
that she may serve those in her service.
May the leaders of the world,
and especially of this land,
know and show that more excellent way,
in which to be spiritually minded
is life and peace.
Help us in times of strife
to anneal the brittle hardness
of our hearts,
that we may be no longer stiff-necked with greed,
and fraught with fear
for status and possessions,
but may honour one another in love,
and seek the common good.

3(c) Bless, O Lord, our Sovereign Queen Elizabeth,
defender of Faith in you.
[May she so reflect your kingship,
that ministers of the Crown,
and all her people,
may rejoice to be ruled
in peace, justice and mercy.]
Guide the Government of this nation,
and the law makers of all nations,
that they may distinguish between need and greed,
and so reward the dedication
of honest and skilled activities
that mankind may honour one another
and seek the common good.

3(d) Bless and guide Elizabeth our Queen
and let the majesty of our nation be
that we follow in the way
of your justice and peace.
We bring before you, in silent contemplation,
the troubled communities of this realm,

. . . .

and strife between nations.

. . . .

Forgive, O Lord, both them and us,
for sins of commission,
for sins of omission,

. . . .

and lead each to honour the other,
and seek the common good.

3(e) Bless and guide Elizabeth our Queen,
[who is so often both source and focus
of the spirit of our nation.]
Give wisdom to all in authority,
especially to those who administer laws
that are challenged
by sections of society.
Constrain us all to listen and to reason,
rather than resort to violence.
Help us to respond to the honour
we see in others,
and to find the opportune occasions
to seek the common good.

3(f) Bless and guide Elizabeth our Queen,
and all the royal family,
[and let their devotion to duty,
love of this nation,
and concern for peoples overseas,
be for us an inspiration,
a pattern and a pride.]
Grant, O Lord, wisdom
to the ministers of the crown,
that they may advise and direct
with the authority won
by willing service.
[Help us to think through the problems
of our evolving society.]
Give us a determined regard for those
who are least able to defend themselves,
and a love of justice and mercy
powerful enough for mankind
to seek to honour one another,
consciously to avoid
divisive strife,
and to seek to promote
the common good.

3(g) Defend, O God, our gracious Queen
in all the pressures and demands
of her position,
[that she may, by your divine appointment,
continue to rule this kingdom
with love and justice.]
May the advice of her ministers,
and the decisions of her judges,
serve to unite us in a merciful purpose.
Help us all to distinguish
between right ambition
and stubborn self-seeking,
between care for the individual
and disregard for the community,
and may all violence
of thought, word and deed
within and between all nations,
be quelled by the engendering of trust,
conceived of honesty out of patience,
to your honour and glory.

3(h) Bless and guide Elizabeth our Queen,
and all the royal family,
[and grant them the gracious presence,
the patience and the concern,
that we expect of them.]
Give wisdom to all in authority,
especially those who have the power
to help the helpless poor,
and the unwillingly unemployed.
Direct this and every nation
in the ways of justice and mercy,
and in the ways of purposeful peace,
that mankind may honour one another,
and seek,
and seek again,
the common good.

3(i) Long live Elizabeth our Queen,
in your grace and favour,
[that she may be a symbol and a sign
of the peace and stability,
and of the justice and mercy,
that we desire for this nation.]
Grant a sufficiency of wisdom
to those in authority,
both great and small,
and courage to apply your wisdom with truth,
and with compassion.
Let not extremes of party political principles
blind those who govern
or motivate those who oppose,
lest we cease to honour one another,
and have no common good to seek.

3(j) Grant, O Lord, to all sovereigns and rulers,
and especially to Elizabeth our Queen,
and all her ministers,
the enlightenment needed to establish and defend
justice and mercy,
peace and benevolence.
Let honesty of purpose be matched
by honesty of practice,
in all levels of administration,
that those who labour with their hands
may respect those who organise and lead,
and work together in companionship
towards a common good.

Lord, in your mercy
Hear our prayer.

4. Our neighbours

4(a) Give grace to our families and friends,
and to all our neighbours,
and especially to those whom we love
but who do not share our faith.
We pray for people who find faith difficult,
for wilful unbelievers,
for those whose honest doubts
are sometimes more real
than their shaky convictions.
We pray for ourselves,
'Lord, I believe; help my unbelief'.

4(b) Give grace to us and to our families,
to those whom we love best,
and who forgive us most.
Grant to our friends and neighbours
strength in need,
comfort in sorrow,
and joy in companionship,
that we all may serve Christ in one another,
and love as he loves us.

4(c) Lord of all grace,
you know the needs of all of us
before we think or ask.
Help us to know those closely linked with us,
not only by name
but by need.
Help us to know ourselves
and to distinguish between our needs
and our desires.
Grant that our families, friends and neighbours
may with us respond to your Holy Spirit,
in loving service to each other.

4(d) We thank you, Lord,
for our families,
for our friends,
and for our neighbours near and far.
Help us to care for them,
as we would wish them to care for us,
and grant us such oneness of purpose
that we are able to serve Christ
in one another,
and both live to love
and love to live.

4(e) We thank you Lord
for families, friends and neighbours,
for the joys of close relationships,
and for all they teach us of your love.
Encourage the young,
support the old,
assist those who care for them,
and those who care for the carers.
Grant to all of us patience,
understanding
and good humour,
and let our service to each other
be patterned on the life of Christ,
in the power of your Holy Spirit.

4(f) Lord of all mankind,
we see our neighbours all about us,
known and unknown,
loved and unloved,
just and unjust,
rich and poor.
Give us grace to seek to know their needs,
to share in their sorrows
and to be in tune with their joy,
that your love may be broadcast
in our love for one another.

4(g) Teach us, good Lord,
to know our neighbours
and be sensitive to their needs,
and to care for our families and friends,
in ways that they can accept and enjoy,
that we may serve you in one another
and share our faith with all mankind.
Give grace to relationships under stress,
especially those within marriage,
and between parents and children,
that the love you have for each one of us
may show in our love for each other.

4(h) Give, O Lord, such grace to us
that we may love our neighbours
as we love ourselves.
Bless our families and friends,
especially those at present in great need,
. . . .
May we, with Jesus Christ as our example,
serve each other with lively joy
and healthy self-abandon,
and thereby learn to love
as Christ loves us.

4(i) Lord, give us the good grace to realise
that our families, friends and neighbours,
are ours because we are theirs.
Help us to be good neighbours to our neighbours,
faithful friends to our friends,
and loving members of our families.
Grant us an abundance of mutuality,
giving to the needy,
and receiving what we need.
Let each one of us
love and serve the other,
and each of us love and serve
our saviour, Jesus Christ.

4(j) Help us to remember, Lord, what you have taught us,
that everybody needs good neighbours,
especially those in broken homes,
in scattered families,
and those who are living alone.
We pray, with particular concern,
for the young and the very young.
Grant to them a sense of being needed,
and of being loved,
if not by those around them,
then most certainly, and always, by you.

Lord, in your mercy
Hear our prayer.

5. The Sick

5(a) Comfort and heal, and strengthen for service,
all those who suffer
in body, mind or spirit,
(especially . . . . . .).
Help them to be open to all the channels
through which your healing grace can flow,
and to be ready to respond
to your lifegiving spirit.
Give them courage and hope in their troubles,
and bring them the joy of your salvation.

5(b) Lord, we know that your loving concern
is for both the sick and the healthy.
Give grace to the healthy who tend the sick
and to the sick who suffer
in body, mind and spirit,
(especially . . . . . .).
Comfort them in their distress,
heal them of their affliction
and by your saving grace
bless them with eternal joy.

5(c) Almighty God,
we bring before you those who suffer
in body, mind or spirit,
(especially . . . . . .).
In their darkest moments, grant them a sense
of your hand holding theirs,
and of your share in their suffering.
Foster within them a healing trust
in those trained to diagnose and treat,
and in the peace-giving power of prayer.
Grant them courage, born of Christ,
hope for the future
and the knowledge and joy
of eternal salvation.

5(d) Lord of all,
in simple trust we present to you
the needs of those who suffer
in body, mind or spirit,
(especially . . . . . .).
Give them a healing sense
of your care and love for them.
Help them to know
when to fight with courage their affliction,
and when to suffer in patience and hope,
and let the joy of your salvation
be their comfort and their peace.

5(e) Almighty and everliving God,
let your healing power make whole
those who suffer,
in body, mind or spirit,
(especially . . . . . .).
Comfort them
and strengthen them.
Grant them confidence
in your unfailing love,
and the trust that leads
to the surprises of joy.

5(f) Merciful Lord,
we commend to your care
those who suffer,
in body, mind or spirit,
(especially . . . . . .).
Show your compassion
to the deaf, the dumb and the blind,
and to the physically handicapped.
Grant relief to those in pain,
particularly the elderly,
and give them patience and courage.
Guide the healthy whose work is with the sick,
that each and all may rejoice
in the knowledge of your salvation.

5(g) Helper of the helpless,
healer of the sick,
we pray for those who suffer,
whatever their affliction,
especially those known to us,
(. . . . . .)
Inspire those who teach and train
doctors and nurses,
guide managers
and administrators
and grant skill, patience and personal well-being
to all who care for the sick.
Give fortitude and good humour
to those who attend to the needs
of the housebound.
And let us not forget that we too, one day,
may be sick and in need of help.

5(h) Give comfort and new health to all who suffer,
in body, mind or spirit,
(especially . . . . . .).
In your great compassion,
relieve those who are chronically ill,
whether in old age
or with diseases and conditions
with no known cure.
Inspire those who seek new remedies
in hospitals, clinics and laboratories.
Let them bring new hope to the sick,
and receive new insights for research.

5(i) We bring before you those who suffer
in body, mind or spirit,
(especially . . . . . .).
Encourage them when their hopes are eroded,
that by their steadfast faith in you
they may bring others into your care.
Help us all to treasure the health we have,
to care for our bodies
as we would have others care for us,
and to do nothing thoughtless or mean
that would endanger the health of others.

5(j) Lord of both the sick and the healthy,
deepen the well-being of the healthy,
and heal the sick in body, mind or spirit,
(especially . . . . . .).
Comfort those who suffer
and give them patience and courage.
Let their hopes be fulfilled
that they may look forward
to a new and richer life
of loving trust in you.
Lift up their hearts,
set firm their resolve,
and bring them the joy
of your salvation.

Lord, in your mercy
Hear our prayer.

6. The dead

6(a) Lord, we remember those who have died
in the faith of Christ,
in our families,
in this Parish,
(especially . . . . . .),
and we remember that we too
must some day die.
Grant us, O Father, a sense of belonging to you,
that with all your children
we may share
in your eternal kingdom.

6(b) Lord of life and death,
we bring to remembrance
those who have died,
especially those known to us,
(. . . . .).
We thank you for your promises
to those who die believing in you.
We commit to your merciful care
those whose faith or disbelief
is known only to you.

6(c) Lord of all life,
before whose face
the generations come and go,
we pray for those who have recently died,
and for those whose anniversary we recall,
(especially . . . . . .).
Grant us a real and spiritual sense
of continuing unity,
being bound together in love,
living the resurrection life of Christ,
and sharing in your eternal kingdom.

6(d) God the ever-loving,
guardian of the dead,
you gave your Son, Jesus Christ,
to suffer and die on the cross,
and to rise again to live in glory.
Hear us as we remember those among us who have died,
(especially . . . . . .).
Grant us all a patient faith,
that we may daily be prepared
for no more days on earth,
and that we may, in the day of the Lord,
enjoy the fullness of your promises
to those who believe.

6(e) Almighty God,
source of all goodness,
in the order of your creation
we must surely die.
We remember those who have recently reached
this stage of their pilgrimage,
(especially . . . . . .).
Grant at the end of time
that we and they may join you
in your eternal kingdom,
where there will be no more death,
neither sorrow,
nor crying,
nor any more pain.

6(f) O Lord our maker,
your mercy endures for ever.
We remember the dead, small and great,
especially those who have recently died.
(. . . . .).
We thank you for the resurrection
of your Son, Jesus Christ,
whereby we are freed
from the fear of death,
and are prepared for the glorious liberty
of your eternal kingdom.

6(g) Almighty and all-knowing god,
source of all compassion and comfort,
our minds and hearts are linked
to those who have recently died,
(especially . . . . . .).
May those who mourn cast their cares on you,
and be consoled by your love.
May their faith, and ours, be purified,
and strengthened,
by reminders of our mortality.
May their hope, and ours, be uplifted
by confidence in your justice and mercy,
and may we all be fulfilled by your grace
as citizens of your eternal kingdom.

6(h) Creator and sustainer of all,
past, present and future,
hear us as we remember those who have died,
(especially . . . . . .).
Your Son, Jesus Christ,
through agony in a garden,
found strength to face,
in the emptiness of the cross,
the feeling of being forsaken.
Fill the emptiness of bereavement
with the fullness of your resurrection life,
that once again the morning stars
may sing together,
and all the sons of God
may shout for joy.

6(i) Lord of the living and the dead,
receive with mercy those who have died,
(especially . . . . . .).
We believe that our death to sin
is followed by our rising again
to the newness of eternal life.
Grant us grace so to live
that we witness to the power
of the resurrection of Jesus.

6(j) Merciful God,
Lord of the living dead,
hear us as we remember those who have died,
(especially . . . . . .).
Help us to remember
that good people do not die,
to live no more,
but more intensely live,
in the glorious freedom
of the company of Christ.
Grant us with all who die in faith,
according to your promises,
a share in your eternal kingdom.

Lord, in your mercy
Hear our prayer.

7. Commendation

7(a) Lord, we rejoice
in the fellowship of (*N.* and) all the saints,
from all the ages.
We thank you for the examples that they provide
and for our sense of unity with them.
Though they and we are many, we are one body.
We commend ourselves
and all Christian people
to your unfailing love.

7(b) With (*N.* and) all your saints
we rejoice in fellowship and communion,
and we share in their lively joy.
Into your gracious keeping and unfailing love
we commend ourselves
and all believers.

7(c) We join with (*N.* and) all the company of saints,
in joy and thanksgiving,
to honour your name
and glory in your salvation.
With all believers, we put our trust in you,
and commend ourselves
to your gracious keeping.

7(d) Grant us, Lord, a deep sense of oneness
with all believers
and with (*N.* and) all your saints.
In unity of spirit and loving fellowship
we join with them in commending ourselves
and all Christian people
to your loving care.

7(e) We thank you for the resurrection life
of all Christian people,
and for the fellowship
of (*N.* and) all your saints.
Trusting in the salvation promises of Jesus our Lord,
we commend to your safe-keeping,
ourselves and all believers,
in faith,
in hope
and in love.

7(f) In unity with (*N.* and) all your saints,
we praise your Holy Name,
and we thank you for all the blessings of this life,
and the promise of the world to come.
In humble trust we commend ourselves,
and all Christian people,
to your unfailing love.

7(g) In knowledge of the example in fellowship
of (*N.* and) all your saints,
and rejoicing in the union with you
of all believers,
we commend ourselves and all Christian people
to the love that you have for all mankind.

7(h) Lord, you have united all believers
in the one communion of your Church.
We rejoice to know that we are one
with (*N.* and) all your saints.
Grant us grace to follow them
in virtuous and godly living.
In humble confidence we commend ourselves,
and all believers,
to your eternal love.

7(i) Our awareness, Lord, of (*N.* and) all your saints
confirms in us that hope of glory
that Jesus promised to those who believe.
Grant that we may follow their example
and share our faith with others.
We place ourselves and all Christian people
in your care,
trusting in your perfect
and ever-present love.

7(j) Almighty and most merciful God,
by the resurrection of your Son Jesus Christ,
we are assured of our fellowship
with (*N.* and) all your saints.
By the gifts of your Holy Spirit,
enable us to follow in their footsteps
so that in joy and thanksgiving
we may commend ourselves
and all believers
to your loving care.

Merciful Father,
accept these prayers
for the sake of your Son,
our Saviour Jesus Christ. Amen.

PART TWO

Prayers and Meditations

Preface to Prayers and Meditations

The principal subjects within these prayers and meditations are more accurately indicated by the individual titles than by the following section headings, which merely serve as a convenient way of grouping the prayers:

8. Experience
9. Belief
10. Suffering
11. Relationships
12. At Communion
13. Occasions
14. Groups

The prayers themselves may be used in any order as may best suit the occasion.

Some images and allusions have been intensified in order to make more vivid certain thoughts that are often understated.

Many of the prayers written in the singular 'I – me – my' bear transfer to the plural 'We – us – our'.

8. Experience

8(a) **Senses**

Lord of the eyes,
    may I not only see
        but look and perceive.

Lord of the nose,
    may I not only smell
        but scent and follow the trail.

Lord of the tongue,
    may I not only taste
        but savour and enjoy.

Lord of the sense of touch,
    may I not only feel
        but probe and discover.

Lord of the ears,
    may I not only hear
        but listen and respond.

8(b) **Beauty**

Blessed and most glorious Trinity,
Maker,
Restorer,
Sustainer
of all creation,

by your Word you introduced us
to all truth,
and by making us in your own image
you enabled us to create and appreciate beauty.

Inspire us to produce and recognise
beautiful works of art.

In our studies of nature
show us the unity in simplicity
and the richness in complexity
of your creation.

In writing
and in our speech,
may our words be the reflected image
of your Word,

so that truth and beauty may bring us
to the eternal goal
and infinite joy
of oneness with you.

8(c) **Enjoying creation**

Master and Lord of all that is true
and all that is pure,

grant us eyes to see
and ears to hear
the messages of creation.

In our various occupations,
and through the diversity
of our abilities,

may we marvel at
the order and the chaos,
the necessity and the chance,
revealed to scientists,

and also enjoy beyond measure
those creative compositions of the arts
that reflect and transmit your image
in which we are being created.

This we pray that we may be fulfilled
in heart and mind and soul,
by your grace and favour.

8(d) **Science**

Almighty God,
master of all the sciences,

your children from their earliest youth
observe with eyes and ears,
discover with their hands,
and experiment as they play.

Thereby they come to know and enjoy
your creation,
they develop their inborn creativity,
and exercise their understanding.

Thus was science,
by your inspiration and revelation,
born and bred,

and with the technology it empowered
mankind learnt to control nature
to our great benefit,
and to abuse nature,
by avarice
and vincible ignorance.

There are so many things we wish to know,
and in the brevity of our lengthening lives
we hasten to advance
the frontiers of our science.

Help us, good Lord, to see our science in context,
to balance its demands
against those of society,
to realise its excitement and its values
in relation to those of the arts,
to parallel and entwine our discoveries
with our discovery of you as Creator,
to shape all our human endeavour
to honour and respect your Creation,
and to display your Holy Spirit in action
in all our needs.

8(e) **Wood**

Most blessed Lord Jesus,
    Master Carpenter of Nazareth,

how often did you see in the grain of wood
    the death and resurrection
        of the leaves of the trees?

and in the knots of wood
    the lifting up of branches
        like the arms of the crucified?

Through your resurrection
    the dead wood of your Cross
        became the Tree of Life,

and the planks of wood blinding our eyes
    could become less even than the specks of sawdust
        we saw in the eyes of others.

Grant, at the end of our earthly life,
    that the wood that encloses our mortal remains
        may become the door to the life
            that you have prepared for us.

8(f) **Stone**

Lord Jesus,

you saw yourself as the stone that the builders rejected.

Through the rolling away of a stone
from a tomb hewn out of rock
you became the main corner-stone.

Let not my heart be stony ground
in receiving the seed of your word,
lest I enter between the upper and lower millstones
of self-condemning disbelief.

Help me to face, like Stephen, the stones
of disapproval of our faith,
and let me be forever self-critical
in casting in my mind the first stone
of disapproval of others.

Make me, like Peter, one of the rocks
upon which your Church continues to be built,

for you are a lively and a precious stone,
and the spiritual rock of our salvation.

8(g) **Water**

Lord Jesus,

your thirst on the Cross
continues today
in thirst for our souls.

Only you can know how deeply each one of us thirsts
for a draught of the water of life.

Draw up water from that well
to refresh us,
to cleanse us,
and to feed our needs.

Show us how to shower on others
the gifts that you have freely given –
our faith, our love and our peace.

And in the troubled sea of this world's cares
buoy us up by your grace,
until we find the calm of trust and hope,
and then once again set sail,
in the wind of your spirit,
to reach the harbour
of heavenly joy.

8(h) **Needs**

Lord of all grace,

grant me the measure of grace
    meet for my needs;

my need to know my needs;

my need not always to need;

my need of your discernment
    to enable me to avoid sin;

my need of your all-permeating mercy,
    that I may be forgiven when I sin;

my need of your gracious power
    sought and unsought,
        craved,
            forgotten
                and impressed:

Grant me evermore
    serenity
        in my need for solitude,
    harmony in affection
        in my need of others,
    and a consuming sense of my creatureliness
        in my need of you,

Creator,
    Saviour,
        and eternal rest.

8(i) **Silence**

Lord of the silence
that leads to your peace,

grant me grace,
in the noisy silence
of unresolved worry,
to open my heart to you.

In the vacuous silence
of thoughtless disregard for others,
invade and destroy my complacency.

In the wounding silence
of burnt-out verbal disagreement,
enlighten my understanding,
and relax my tension.

In the emphatic silence
of pauses in music and speech,
heighten my attention
and let significance be revealed.

In the restless silence
of a sleepless night,
implant the seeds of prayer.

In the elected silence
of emergent meditation,
purify my imagination,
disarm the doubts with which I skirmish,
and illuminate my innermost being.

In the speechless silence of a quiet faith,
in the pulse-beat silence of realised love,
and in the seminal silence of unalloyed joy,

accept my humble and hearty thanks,
for all your goodness
and loving kindness,
to me and to all mankind.

8(j) **Sleep**

Blessed Lord Jesus,
    shepherd of your sheep,

restore me
    in the self-abandonment of sleep,

compose my mind
    in the stillness of forgiveness,

deepen my affections
    in the calm of trust,

relax my limbs
    in unwilled inactivity,

and purpose my prayers
    to serve you afresh
        in the morning.

9. Belief

9(a) Faculties

Lord of my mind,
may I not only think
but wonder and stand in awe.

Lord of my heart,
may I not only like
but love and trust.

Lord of my will,
may I not only seek
but find and seek again.

Lord of my speech,
may I not only say
but keep my word and do.

Lord of my prayer,
may I not only wish
but worship and be still.

9(b) The Way, the Truth and the Life

Lord Jesus Christ,
Master among mankind,

you are the Way,
the Truth,
and the Life.

Create within me

a heart that is large enough
to support a life
of uplifting love
and masterly service,

a mind that is humble enough
to glory in the truth,
of reasoned faith
and vital paradox

and a will that is strong enough
to keep me in the way
of honour,
justice
and mercy,

that I may be united in eternal peace
by and in your name.

9(c) **Glory**

Almighty God,

in the often drab excitement of my ways,

renew within me a daunting sense
    of the glory of glory.

In awe and silence
    feed the hunger of my soul,
    transcend the rationality of my mind,
    speak through the ineffable,

and in the sublime fire of faith
    purify me for union with you,

in the name of Jesus,
    to your honour and glory.

9(d) **Choosing**

Lord of all being,

with your freedom to choose
you chose to make me in your image
free to choose.

When first I chose to follow you
I believed the choosing and commitment
to be fully and solely mine.

But as I began to know you,
the truth burst through
that you chose me.

From my point of view I do the choosing
and in the measure that I see things
from your point of view
you do the choosing.

Lord, I glory in this paradox of faith
and pray that what I do and what I witness
may be used by your Holy Spirit
to bring others to choose
to follow you,

and that they may know
with what love and forgiving
you choose to call
both them and me.

9(e) **Children of our time**

Lord of us all, younger and older,

we are children of our time,
even as the Israelites,
the early Christians,
the Reformers,
and scientists in every age,
were children of their time.

Scientists research your creation
and investigate the image in which they are made.

We cannot believe
that they discover
things that are in essence evil.

In sadness we confess
that some applications of their discoveries
are against your will.

In thankfulness we praise you
for the many manifestations of science
that have improved our life on Earth.

Grant us grace to see afresh your work
of creation, salvation and inspiration,
and the mystery of your being,
in language, images and explanations
that agree with the knowledge and understanding
at present revealed to us.

Help us humbly to accept that there are,
while yet we live on Earth,
depths we cannot fathom
and heights we cannot reach.

Grant that in the final fulfilment
we shall be united with you,
and see all things
in the clear light and glory
of eternity.

9(f) **Creation**

Almighty and all-knowing God,

by your Word, and with instant number,
    you created, and do now create and recreate,
        all that is and will be.

By your Incarnation
    and emptying of self,
        even unto death,
you cancel for ever the debt
    of mankind's ill-chosen self-expression.

By your Holy Spirit
    you grant us the grace to grow
        towards the riches of our true humanity.

We see you as the author and editor
    of all the discoveries of science,
and tutor supreme
    in all the master classes of the arts.

Grant that we may never close our minds,
    nor harden our hearts,
to the marvels of creation
    presented for our understanding,
or to the mysteries that restore and express
    your divine image in us.

Through humility and discernment
    correct and make just our prejudice.

Through meditation and worship
    sow the seeds of healthy exhilaration,
and unite us
    and all your children
        in our search for truth.

9(g) **Evolution**

Almighty God, source of all that is,

by your Word and in your Wisdom
this universe has developed
from chaos into beauty,
stars have evolved and died,
and planets have changed their form.

You have shown to us that our planet Earth is endowed
with the marvellously precise potential for life,
engendered in its intricate splendour
at the earliest moments of creation.

A glorious variety of living creatures has been produced
through generations of evolution,
in which birth, procreation and death
are essential ingredients.

All this you have revealed to us
through the inspiration of scientists,
who seek and find.

Now we knock,
and would have opened unto us,
the meaning of life and death
in the incarnation of your Son,
in his death and resurrection
and in mankind's salvation.

Grant us humility, perseverance and patience
in our continuing search,

that we may love you with all our mind,
proclaim your truth to our neighbours
and love them as we love ourselves,

to your honour and glory.

9(h) **Survival of the fittest**

Lord of the process of creation,

we see in nature the preservation of the best,
    the fittest to survive.

But our consciences and natural love
    drive us to seek out and to care for
        the weak and disabled,
            those least able to survive.

In sacrifices to you we feel constrained
    to offer up our best,
        as did Jesus on the Cross,
            the Lamb without blemish.

We see these caring and sacrificial acts
    as a measure of your image in mankind.

Help us as we try, with this in mind,
    to fathom our faith in Jesus,
        and recognise the source of our salvation.

Grant us to share the triumph
    that Jesus accomplished
        in giving himself.

Show us that in sacrificing our best
    we preserve the best,

for those who give of their best to others
    are the fittest
        for the survival of mankind.

9(i) **Sin and Death**

Lord of life,
source of all truth,

in the evolution of mankind,
physical death is seen
as an essential and inevitable part
of the pattern of your creation.

This understanding of the origin of physical death
is very different
from that of the Jews
to whom Jesus spoke,
and from that of your Church
through many centuries.

I know I am diminished by my sin,
and without forgiveness and reconciliation
I shall die a spiritual death.

In my seeking to fathom and relate
sin and death and salvation,
help me to distinguish, as did Jesus,
between parables, with their figures of speech,
and plain speaking.

Through physical death came Man,
through Man came spiritual death.

Through the physical death and resurrection of Jesus,
came the spiritual resurrection
of those who believe.

Help me in my response
to love you with all my heart,
with all my mind,
and with all my soul

that your message for mankind may attract and hold
this present generation

to your greater glory.

9(j) **Life after death**

Lord Jesus,

you entered fully into mankind's mortality,
    and triumphed over death.

Grant me such a measure of eternal life
    as a member of the kingdom of heaven,
that I may at the last be clothed
    in a spiritual body,
        fit to ascend to you,
    in purity of mind,
    in true purpose of will,
    and in grace-given sanctity of soul,

filled,
    fulfilled
        and brimming over

with the Holy Spirit.

9(k) **Freewill**

Almighty and all-knowing God,

I struggle in my mind
    to marry your eternal knowledge
        to the freedom that I find in my will,
            and to my knowledge of right and wrong.

Let not my lack of comprehension of your omniscience
    weaken and corrupt my conscience.

Let me not freely choose to say
    I am not free to choose
        the good.

Deepen in me the shame of wilful sin,
    drive home the heartache of neglect
        and accent the agony of omission.

Above all the storms of guilt,
    make me vividly aware
        of the forgivability
            of my foolish ways,

that in the unfathomable mystery
    of the saving work of Christ, your Son,

I may find the peace
    that needs no understanding.

9(l) **Hallowed be your name**

God, our Father
hallowed be your name,
your will be done,
in your Church,
by both men and women.

Guide those who wish to call you
both Father,
and Mother.

Help us all to intercede in love
for all who acknowledge you,
and for all who worship you.

When we favour extreme but honest expressions
and exclusive but telling images,
whether recent or ancient,
let us use them so wisely and lovingly
that they offend not your children.

Grant us a proper humility and patience
in the face of spiritual experiments,

lest we offend against your Holy Spirit
by living with closed minds
rather than by recognising and living
the truth at both extremes.

9(m) Other religions

Lord of all holiness,

we believe and trust in you,
one God of us all.

Your revelation throughout the ages
has guided the evolution of belief.

Help us to identify truth held in common
in the religions of mankind,
truth of yourself
as creator and sustainer,
and as eternal source,
of loving forgiveness
and peace in fulfilment.

For Christians you have spoken
through the patriarchs and prophets
and in and through your Son,
Jesus,
Christ and Lord.

Jesus had many things to say to his disciples,
but they could not bear them at that time.
Enable us, today's disciples, to listen to your words,
and show us where we have been lacking in caution
in overelaborate creeds,
and in merciless anathemas,
that divide your people.

Strengthen in us, and in all religions,
the eternal truths that bind us to you,
and should bind us together,
and grant us grace
to practise tolerance
in loving and suffering patience,
and to avoid the discord and violence
deriving from the belief
that your revelation is completed.

This we ask that your name may be held holy
and that your Spirit may unite all who worship you.

9(n) **May I be sure**

Jesus the Christ, Son of God, Saviour,

enfold me in your being,

that I may be sure I am with you
in all I think
and all I say
and all I do.

When I am deeply concerned,
may I be sure
that it is your concern.

When I suffer pain,
may I be sure
that I pattern myself on your suffering.

When I know joy and peace,
may I be sure
that they are your joy and peace
to be shared with others.

When I love,
may I be sure
that the love springs from you
and returns to you.

When I am enriched by enthusiasm,
may I be sure
that I share in your Spirit.

When I pray,
may I be sure
that I enter not into temptation
but watch and pray with you.

9(o) **On the other hand**

Lord Jesus,
Word of God,

speak to us through your Holy Spirit
and let not conflict of opinion,
in Church or in State,
destroy the bonds of unity
that we need to defend.

When we clasp our hands in prayer,
the fingers on one hand
point to the left,
and on the other hand
point to the right.

Let this be an ever present symbol,
reminding each of us of the need to strive
to see the other's point of view,
both before and after deciding
to support one, or the other,
or to live in tension and balance with both.

When we unclasp our hands from prayer
and use them for our work
may both together perform their practical tasks
for the right-handed,
and the left-handed,
and for the ambidextrous,
to their satisfaction and pleasure.

And when in thanksgiving and praise
we put our praying hands palm to palm
may the fingers on both of our hands
point to you
source, transmitter and receiver
of honour and glory.

9(p) **Humility**

Lord of the knowledge and understanding
that we have of ourselves,

grant us the grace to be humble.

Guard us from the humility that is false,
denying the very gifts
that you have entrusted to us,
with which we should bear witness.

Let us not pretend to be humble in our hearts
when we are lazy in our wills
and unthinking in our beliefs.

Make us humble in our expressions of faith
lest we claim to know revealed truth
that so conflicts with the convictions of others
that both of us offend
against the mystery of your Being.

In our deliberations with other communities of your Church
make us particularly aware of the awesome constraints
of formal creeds and exclusive doctrines
concerning your Godhead in Trinity
and the process of our salvation,

lest in the over-confidence of an inert faith
we lose the inheritance of the meek
not only on Earth
but in Heaven.

10. Suffering

10(a) Suffering

Lord Jesus,
it was part of your suffering on the cross
to feel that you were forsaken.

When we suffer pain or disability,
be with us when we feel forsaken,
and when we doubt your loving kindness.

Help us to acknowledge the mystery
of non-intervention of the Father
on your behalf,
and so accept divine non-intervention
on our behalf.

Although we do not understand
the necessity of suffering in your creation,
whether in disease,
or in natural disaster,
transform our confusion into re-dedication of our wills,
and grant us determination to win through,
even when the pain or disability
threatens to continue till we die.

Let us when we suffer the smaller discomforts
use them to relate to those who suffer severely,
so that with greater sensitivity and perception
we may be agents of your loving concern.

In our love for each other we find meaning in life,
and in your anguish and death on the cross
we find the meaning of your love for us.

(continued)

Help us to accept suffering as an opportunity
both to be united through your suffering
with all those who suffer,
and to share in their triumphs and their love.

Through suffering give us grace to know more fully
the glory of that resurrection life
won for us through your cross
and your triumph over death.

10(b) **Temptation**

Lord Jesus,

you knew what it was to be tempted,
not only in the desolation of the desert,
but also in the beauty of a garden.

When I am tempted to sin,
tempt me to do the good.

Feed choices to my conscious thoughts,
guide me to choose the right,
and stiffen my will
to reject the wrong.

Let me not harbour,
nor entertain,
temptation,

lest the transitory false pleasure that it gives
should weaken my initial resolve
to resist and defeat its treachery.

Lead me, I entreat you,
not into temptation
but in and through temptation,

that I may be triumphant in tribulation,
by the power of your Holy Spirit.

10(c) **Discontent**

Lord Jesus,
exemplar and friend,

help me to distinguish between
divine
and devilish
discontent.

Let my discontent with the second-rate,
in thoughts, and words and actions,
prepare me for invasion
by the power of your Holy Spirit.

Grant me the wisdom, courage and means
to identify and improve standards of behaviour
that fail to match
your way
your truth
and your life,
both in others and in myself.

When, in my selfishness, I feel and show
unbridled discontent
for petty discomforts,

when I harbour and encourage
obsessional beliefs
in personal rights and privileges,

give me a sense
of the true proportions of hope,
and of the peace in strife
that replaces evil exaggeration
by charitable assessment,

and let me count the many, many blessings
for which your name be praised.

10(d) **Sleeplessness**

Lord Jesus,
    master of minds,
        shepherd of souls,

teach me how to cope with the plunderers of my sleep,
    the din of overactive thoughts,
        worry about the past,
        anxiety about the future,
    the sudden noise of thunder,
        the murmur of machines,
    the aches and pains of age and injury,
    and the guilt of neglected reconciliation.

Comfort me
    in the unrelated emptiness
        of unuttered silence,
    and in the disorienting and blinding darkness
        that has no visible ray of hope.

Temper my distress
    in dry and humid heat
    and in cheerless cold.

And when all that I know and understand
    appears to be propitious for my slumber
        and still I do not sleep,

help me to think of your other sheep,
    whom I count as my friends,

that I and they may be enfolded in eternal rest
    both now and hereafter,

to your honour and glory.

10(e) **Hunger**

God the compassionate, God the merciful,
we bring before you the hunger
of people in many lands.

Forgive and reform those who make barren
the lands of the needy,
by culpable neglect,
greedy exploitation
and factional conflicts.

Help us to think through
what we should do for the victims,
both as individuals by giving what we can
and as countries by planning aid and support.

Enable those who know how to manage
to teach those who don't,
that assisted by the sharing of resources
they may learn how to help themselves.

Guide us, with determination,
to avoid the shameful scandal
of mountains of food
and lack of transport.

Convince those who have the means
to give yet more generously,
so that relief agencies may be enabled
to respond to sudden need,
especially after natural disasters.

In your mercy spare us
from drought and flood and earthquake,
and extremes of heat and cold,
and teach us where and how to live,
as you would have us live,
on this your world.

Stimulate our consciences, this and every day,
feed our imaginations,
and give us the wills to respond,
that by loving care for others
we may witness to your care for us all.

10(f) **Depression**

Lord of all creation,

who in the fullness of your incarnation,
    and on the cross,
knew what it was to feel forsaken,
    and therefore to know
        the despair of the depressed,

reveal at least the fringe of your glory
    to those in distress of mind.

Where they see darkness,
    let them see that it is your darkness
        in which you hold their hand,
    and let there be stars to guide them.

Where they see difficulties,
    let them remember with renewed hope
        the ways of escape and triumph.

Where they see evil,
    let there be forgiveness
        and the invasion of your grace.

Where they have an unremitting hatred of themselves,
    and they are afraid of being afraid,
        let them know once again
            the power of your love for them.

And when the depression has lifted,
grant them
    the wisdom to be aware of weakness,
    grace to avoid the valleys of vulnerability,
    and such love, joy and peace
        as they can both receive and bear
            and henceforth give

in and through your name.

10(g) **Ups and downs**

Blessed Lord Jesus,
    Word of all creation,

in your wisdom you fashion mountains and hills
    and form the rivers and their valleys.

Grant me grace
    not only to live on the hilltops
        of love, joy, peace
            and all manner of goodness,

but also to know your presence
    in the valleys of frustration,
        disappointment,
            and depression,
    and in the mire of unrepented sin.

Help me to hold fast to your rod and your staff
    in the valley of the shadow of death,
        and to know that you are holding me,

that at the last I may,
    with all your saints,

shout for the joy of fulfilment
    in oneness with you.

11. Relationships

11(a) Loving my neighbour

Jesus, Lord of love,

you have told us to love one another
as you have loved us,
and I am commanded to love my neighbour as myself.

When I so often do not like or love myself,
is it because
I so often do not love my neighbour?

Grant me grace
to share in others' interests
even when they are not my own,
to suffer my neighbour's weaknesses
and thereby see my own,
to listen and be patient
even when I am busy or tired,
to give more of the time that you have given
which now I give to self,
to sow in my neighbour's sadness
the seeds of joy,
to radiate peace
where there is turmoil,
to strengthen faith
where there is doubt,
and to be a channel
for the fruits of your resurrection.

Help me by forgiving my neighbour
to learn to forgive myself,

that thereby I may know more truly
the power of your forgiving.

Help me not to love myself for myself,
but because I love my neighbour,

and thereby express your love
for both my neighbour and myself,

to your honour and glory.

11(b) **Families**

Lord of creation,

in your loving wisdom
you caused both men and women
to inhabit the gardens
and the wildernesses
of this world.

We thank you
for the depths and intensities
of love in marriage,
and for the joys and surprises
of children.

Grant an abundance of grace and patience
to partners facing fractious
and divisive
difficulties.

Unwind the tangles
of unfaithful relationships.

Strengthen and support
those who live alone,
and those who endeavour to be
both father and mother
to their children.

Enrich and sanctify
the divorced who marry again.

Hallow into wholeness
the contradictory actions
and confusing charades
of children,

so that they, and we, may marvel at
the healing power of forgiving,
and the fullness of lives
committed to your providential care.

11(c) **Forgiving**

Father forgive me,
  for I know so often what I do,
if not before,
  or during my offence,
    then most certainly thereafter.

Forgiving Father,
  when I know not what I do,
convince my conscience
  of your displeasure,
that I may convict myself,
  and be prepared
    for true repentance.

Help me to forgive
  those who offend and sin against me,
that I may be fit to ask, and to receive,
  your forgiveness.

When I ask others to forgive,
  and they forgive me not,
grant me your forgiveness,
  and grace to forgive myself.

Teach me how to know your forgiveness,
  in the fullness of mankind's salvation,
that I may forget my guilt,
  yet be resolved to remember,
    and avoid,
      the cause of my offence.

Let the freshness of forgiveness
  lift my heart,
    and renew my hope,
that love, joy and peace
  may once more unite us all,
    as members of your Church,
      the family of the forgiven,
        and of the forgiving,
with Jesus as our Saviour.

11(d) **Money**

Jesus, Lord of all,

it was against the misuse of money in the Temple
that you showed both violence and anger.

Grant that we,
members of your Church,
temples of the new covenant,
and of your Holy Spirit,

may gather and give money
with wisdom,
simplicity,
generosity
and care.

Help us to be good stewards
of all the fruits of your creation
and of the labours of mankind.

Help us in our control and influence of nature
not to set profit before providence
nor to neglect need by falling into greed.

By your forgiveness and grace
bring us to the dynamic peace of Heaven,
where there is neither giving
nor receiving
of money.

11(e) **Rich and Poor**

Creator and sustainer of both rich and poor,

let not material riches,
    nor poverty,
        hide your eternal majesty.

Whatever the origin of wealth,
    let it not lead
        to a sense of self-sufficiency,
        and flaunting reliance
            on material things.

Whatever the cause of poverty,
    let it not lead
        to degradation of self,
        and despairing desire
            for earthly possessions.

Let us all,
    rich and poor and in-between,
find fulfilment
    in self-abandonment to your divine providence,

so that the gifts of your Holy Spirit
    may make us in our hearts
        as rich as Jesus.

11(f) **Love and Joy**

Lord Jesus,
author of all love and joy,

grant that in our prayer
the marriage of mind and emotion
may have issue in love, joy and peace,
and may deepen devotion.

Help us to open ourselves
to your Holy Spirit
by consciously abandoning
sterile and joyless attitudes.

Keep us ever aware, in silent contemplation,
of the awesome uplifting holiness
and joyfulness
of the means of grace.

May we share with each other
mutual delight,
kindly good humour,
eye-to-eye contentment
and all that leads to loving care
and fullness of joy.

May we see in love and joy
a part of you
and of your image
in which we have been
and are being made.

12. At Communion

12(a) **Easter Day**

Most glorious Trinity,
Creator,
Saviour,
and Comforter,

on this Easter Day we join in the dawn chorus
of all your saints and children,
in singing praises and thanksgivings.

May we ever hold onto and proclaim
the power and promise
of your resurrection.

Help us by daily and sacramental grace
to resurrect the patchy deadness of our souls,
and to ascend in mind and will
above the temptations and dis-ease
of mortal concern
and faithless worry.

Grant that Easter joy
may show itself
to all whom we meet,
and may radiate
the good news
of mankind's salvation
and the pattern
for mankind's fulfilment.

12(b) **Sacrifice**

Lord of this sacrifice
of praise and thanksgiving,

renew in the hearts and minds of mankind
the meaning of sacrifice.

So often we see sacrifice
as negative rather than positive,
as self-denying rather than self-fulfilling,
as giving up rather than taking on board.

The burnt offerings of your chosen people,
however sweet their savour,
and the slaughter of lambs,
with sprinkling of blood
seem to us at first to be the naivities of the past
in placation of a demanding deity.

Then in this communion we are arrested
by the body and blood of Jesus,
the Lamb of God,
that takes away the sin of the world.

Help us to recognise
the pattern of your revelation,
the role of your chosen people,
and the need for a visible sign
in sacramental worship.

We see in Jesus, your Son,
the very best of mankind
who in sacrifice gave of his best,
his very self.

Help us to give of our best
the best of our praise and thanksgiving,
the best of all we have.

Grant us to know that in giving of our best
we become our best,
fit to receive the power of your Spirit,
lifting our best into better.

12(c) The New Covenant

Lord of the New Covenant
    mediated by Jesus,

grant us grace to realise
    that it takes two to make a covenant.

Your Covenant with Israel,
    with the promise of land and protection
        for your chosen people,
set for them standards of behaviour,
    inscribed on tablets of stone
        revered in the Ark of the Covenant,
and was sealed by the blood of sacrifice.

Help us through this Holy Communion
    to honour the New Covenant
        inscribed in our hearts,
            sealed by the blood of Jesus,
                whose cup this is.

Your promise to us is eternal life,
    here and now and forever,
        through forgiveness of sin.

Our promise to you is to love you
    with all our mind,
        with all our heart,
            and with all our strength,
and our neighbours as ourselves.

Help us to see the bread of life
    and the cup of the New Covenant
        as visible and outward signs
            of inward and spiritual grace.

and bind us together Lord in love,
    each with the other
        and both with you,
with cords that cannot be broken.

12(d) **Bread**

Lord of the harvest,
risen from the buried seed,

give us today the grain to grind
to make our bread for tomorrow.

Leaven the lumpy heaviness
of our self-indulgence.

Let the pallid dough
of our half-baked ideas
be raised and made crisp and wholesome
by the steady warmth
of dedicated imagination.

Feed us and all your children
with the oven-fresh bread
of eternal life.

And when we dine with you
on bread and wine
at your holy table,
fill our hearts with thankfulness
for your loving mercies,
and make us one body
as we eat of the one bread.

12(e) **Wine**

Lord of the cup of blessing

by your forgiving grace
    you gladden the hearts of mankind.

In your creative wisdom
    you provide flowers and fruits
        for our pleasure and sustenance,

and from the fruit of the vine
    you have shown us how to prepare
        wine for well-being
            and for healing.

From the ferment of our inner arguments
    clarify, mature and decant
        the vintage wine of faith.

From the heat of our passions
    distill the strong spirit
        of your own incomparable compassion.

Let our remembrance of you in bread and wine
    be both the receiving of grace
        and the giving of thanks
            in the mystery of communion.

12(f) **Crosses**

Jesus, our Saviour,
Lord of the cross,
Lord over death,
risen, ascended, triumphant,

guide my eyes to see the crosses that abound around me,
to remind me of your work on Earth.

In the spars of windows;
Lord Jesus, source of knowledge and understanding,
let your light illuminate my mind.

In the panels of doors;
when I knock, open to me your revelation,
in the Bible, the Church, the arts and the sciences.

On electricity pylons;
transmit to me the power of your Holy Spirit,
and give me the energy to do your will.

On tiled walls
protect me from the stains of sin,
and wipe away my offences.

On weather vanes;
show me the cardinal points of faith and doctrine,
and the direction of the wind of your Spirit.

On tombstones and graves;
Lord Jesus, when I die,
may I know the promise of your resurrection,
and rejoice with all your children,
in union with you.

13. Occasions

13(a) Nature conservation

Jesus, our Lord,
master scientist of minds and souls,

lift up and enlighten
the fallen minds of mankind.

Let us in our understanding and control of nature,
assess the benefits of technology
in relation to its inseparable risks,
and never direct technology to evil ends.

Let us not plan on Earth
what we would not wish
to admit to you in Heaven.

Let not neglect, or blindness of the busy,
produce pollution,
or threaten the destruction
of this beautiful world.

For the sake of us all,
those who care,
and those who don't,
we ask this in your name.

13(b) **The balance of nature**

Lord of the balance of nature,
healing mankind's distortion
of the harmony in your creation,

help us to respect and conserve
the delicate robustness of our planet.

Give us the knowledge and understanding,
the desire and the will,
to avoid the catastrophic consequences
that threaten to overtake us.

Forgive us for the increasing contamination
of air and soil and water,
produced by ignorance and neglect in the past
and wilful exploitation in the present,
and made more difficult to correct
by the planned continuation
of our dangerous habits.

Help us to see the whole world
as the single community of mankind,
and give us the grace and common sense
to cooperate with each other,
and thereby recognise the true purpose of our lives
in learning the meaning of love,
in union with you.

13(c) **Recreation**

God of creation,

who by your inspiration of holy men
ordained in each week
a holy day of recreation,

grant us such respect
for the needs of our bodies
that we may renew their strength
and magnify their well-being.

Direct and redirect
our minds and motives.

Cleanse our consciences
by your merciful forgiving,

and purify, sweeten and feed
the essence of our souls.

that we may exercise ourselves
in faith, hope and love,
and be made ready to receive
the gifts of your Spirit.

13(d) **Musical talent**

Lord of our life,
and God of our salvation,

we thank you for all the talents
that you have given us,

those that we enjoy
and those that give enjoyment to others.

Especially we thank you for music,
which knows no barriers of language,
and conveys what words cannot express,

and for song and dance
which in their manifold forms
delight both young and old.

Help us to use all our talents
to your honour and glory.

13(e) **Computers**

Almighty God,

your Spirit has led scientists
by inquisitive endeavour,
deeper understanding
and determined application,
to invent and multiply computers.

Grant us now the wisdom and courage needed
to control their exploitation.

Let your Church lead those concerned
in maintaining the dignity,
and sanctifiability,
of mankind,
above the menace of machines
installed for greed and graft.

Help us to rejoice
in all the good things provided by computers
in our daily lives,
in discovering more about your creation,
and in the cooperative control of nature
by magnaminous means
towards ends with eternal values.

Make holy and just our thoughts,
edit and clear our memories
and restore the true functions of our minds.

Let not the loops of self-indulence
hinder the flow of your grace,
nor let the obsession of programmed performance
deface the individual soul,

so that, at the end,
we may be free from error
and be integrated
and united with you.

13(f) **The Olympics**

God our maker,
and lord of all life,

we see competition in every corner of creation,
with triumph for the strong
and, according to their swiftness,
success for the hunter
or escape for the quarry.

Be present in the arenas of the Olympics,
to bring out the best in mankind.

Let the reward of those who win,
and the comfort of those who lose,
be the pleasure of participation in the games,
the encouragement of friendship between nations
and the sharing of the gifts of your Holy Spirit,

through Jesus Christ,
our Lord and Saviour,
manager and trainer of our souls.

13(g) **Moving house**

Blessed Lord Jesus,

who in your self-emptying incarnation
experienced the creaturely limitations
of mankind,

and did thereby enter fully into the uncertain security
of families and homes,

lift up the hearts of those cast down
by the trials and traumas of sudden change
in their pattern of living.

Help those who move from one house to another
and who are bereft of nearby friends
and supportive fields of reference.

Let not the loss of visible and tangible convention
inhibit the birth and growth
of a new richness of relationships
to people,
to buildings,
to gardens,
to village, town or city
and to landscape, sky or sea.

Grant them grace to be strengthened in their souls
by recognition of over-dependence
on the transient pleasure of this life.

Let them, like their new dwellings,
be swept clean in their consciences,
redecorated in their minds,
and refurnished in their faith.

Grant them strength to re-establish
the routines of living
that they have lost,

and let their reordered lives confess
    the beauty of your peace,

that at the last they may be more than ready
    to move to your Father's house,
        in which there are many mansions.

14. Groups

14(a) Opening a discussion group

(i)

Lord Jesus,
source and transmitter
of all we need to know,

switch on the receiver in our minds,
tune our affections,
and control the tone and volume
of our discussion,

that we may learn from the thoughts of each other,
by the indwelling of your Holy Spirit,

for yours is the kingdom,
the power,
and the glory,

for ever and ever.

(ii)

Visit we beseech you, O Lord,
this group.

Drive far from it
all idle and contentious thoughts.

Let your Holy Spirit guide our speech,
and control our silence,
that we may listen each to the other,

and may your blessing be upon us evermore,

through Jesus, Christ, our Lord.

14(b) **Closing a discussion group**

(ii)

Lord Jesus,

we thank you for your presence with us,
guiding our worthy thoughts
and forgiving those best forgotten.

Lead and guide us in all we do,
that we may so pursue our daily lives
that they may be witnesses to your loving care
for all your children.

Bind us together Lord, within your Church,

and by your Holy Spirit enable us to speak
to the hearts and minds
of those who do not acknowledge you.

Be with us, Lord,
until we meet again.

(iii)

Lord, you have been listening
with more care and perception,
love and understanding,
than we can muster.

Help us to remember,
and absorb into our being,
whatever we have heard or thought
that accords with your nature,
and your will.

Send us out,
with peace and joy,
to live our lives
to your honour and glory.

14(c) **Opening a Bible study**

(i)

Speak to us, Lord,
through all the channels
of your divine communication:

through the prophets and leaders of Israel,
revealing their evolving image of yourself;

through our Saviour, Jesus Christ,
revealing the pure image of yourself,
giving us a living example to follow
by the power of your Holy Spirit;

through the inspired interpretations
over many generations,
of your multi-faceted Church;

and through your impartial revelation
of the beauties and mysteries of your creation
to all honest and diligent enquirers.

Help us to study the Bible
in the context of the beliefs and knowledge
of its writers,
and in the context of the needs and understanding
of this present age,

that we may by your Word
draw all mankind unto you.

(ii)

Holy Spirit,
teacher, tutor and companion,

lead us in the study of the Bible
to distinguish between literal truth
and parables and poetry.

Reveal to us the richness
of alternative interpretations,
that each of us may recognise the message,
and be in tune with the inspiration,
that meets our individual needs.

Let not our differences of understanding
undermine our union with you,
and with each other,
but rather let them be, by your special grace,
a cause for rejoicing
in Christ's resurrection life.

14(d) **Closing a Bible study**

(i)

Ever present God,

we thank you
for what we have shared,
for what we have learned,
for our common experience of revelation
and for our individual insights.

Grant that our time together
may lead to a step forward
in our pilgrimage of faith.

Help us to believe the fullness of your truth,
that we may practise what we believe,
and may witness by what we practise,
and may bring others to you
by what we witness.

(ii)

Holy Spirit,
source of grace,

receive our humble and hearty thanks
for the privilege of studying your word.

Grant us peace in our hearts and minds,
joy in our companionship,
and determination to witness to others.

In your wisdom,
make us as wise as we can bear,

and let the vision of Christ's purpose
dwell within us,
motivate our actions
and bring us to fulfilment
in the life eternal.